Also by Edgar Wollstone

Chronicles of Spy Ladies

Miss Fatale - Greatest World War II Female Spy, In a Fly : Virginia Hall's Finger Prints over Allies' World War II Victory

Agent Sonya - The Lady of Espionage : Astounding Story of The Spy Ursula Kuczynski

Life & Legacy In a Fly

Churchill's Better Half - Clementine Churchill : Life and Legacy of Winston Churchill's Wife, Clementine Churchill, in a Fly

Sniper Chronicles

Simo Hayha - The Deadliest Sniper In Military History : War Story of The Deadliest Sniper In Military History, In a Fly

Lady Death - The Beauty With a Sniper : Fascinating Tale of Lyudmila Pavlichenko, The Deadliest Female Sniper in History

Carlos Hathcock - Vietnam's Most Wanted Sniper : The Sniper's Extraordinary Engagements During Vietnam War, in a Fly

Killing Silently : American Sniper Chris Kyle's Lethal Moments
Sniper of Vietnam War : The Shots of Marine Sniper Chuck Mawhinney, In a Fly
500+ Kills - Sniper Ivan Sidorenko : WWII Hero of the Soviet Union
Deadly Sniper Duels - The War Story of Controversial Duel Between The Soviet Sniper Expert Vasily Zaitsev And The Mysterious Top Nazi Sniper in WW2

Titan Fails

Titan Fails - Vietnam War : How & Why America Lost the Vietnam War

War Classics In a Fly

Battle of the Atlantic, in a Fly : Long 2,075 days of War in World War 2
Battle of Midway, WWII Naval Battle in a Fly : Captivating Read on the Motives, Strategies, Tactics and the Winning Events of the Decisive World War II Battle
Battle of Okinawa, in a Fly : A Chilling Epitome on the Bloodiest Battle in Pacific Theater of World War 2
D-DAY, in A Fly : Deceptive Operation Bodyguard, Gruesome Battle of Normandy and the Aftermath
American Civil War, in a Fly

World War II Military Operations

Operation Mincemeat : A WWII British Deception Operation
Laconia Incident - A High-Risk Military Rescue Operation of WWII Under The Line of Fire
Operation Vengeance - Killing Admiral Yamamoto : The Stunning Top Secret WWII Military Operation, In a Fly

Standalone

Maya Angelou's Life In a Fly : Retrospective Voyage Through the Life of Maya Angelou
Yoshie Shiratori, The Grand Jailbreaker : Heart-Touching Story of a Japanese Jailbreak Expert
Dawn After Twilight : Industrial Rising of Japan After WW2
Ben L Salomon, The Lone Machine Gunner : A Valiant Story from WW2, in a Fly
Manoeuvres, Shots and Drops - Dive Bomber Pilot Richard Halsey Best In World War 2
Hitler's Girls : Captivate Spy Stories of WWII Female Nazi Spies
Oppenheimer - The Atomic Intelligence : Inside The Brilliant Mind of Robert Oppenheimer, Father of The Atomic Bomb
Puerto Rican Rambo - Story of Jorge Otero Barreto, The Most Decorated U.S. Soldier Of The Vietnam War : Sergeant Rock, In a Fly
Pull It Like Chesty : Life and Legacy of America's Most Decorated Marine, Chesty Puller
The Dark Encounters in Vietnam : Spine-Chilling Horror Stories From Vietnam War
The Other Side of Agent Zigzag : Greatest Double Agent of World War II, Eddie Chapman, In a Fly

The Real Peaky Blinders : Gangster Story of The Actual Peaky Blinders, From Origin to Fall
Niihau Incident : When a Japanese Pilot After Pearl Harbor Attack Crash-Landed on a Hawaiian Island
The Bermuda Triangle of Transylvania, - Hoia Forest -
The Forgotten War Heroes of Vietnam War - Volume II : War Stories of William Pitsenbarger, William Maud Bryant & Jimmie E. Howard
The Forgotten War Heroes of Vietnam War - Volume I : War Stories of George “Bud” Day, Drew Dix, & Jay Vargas
WW2 in Meth - Battling Hallucinations, Enemy Soldiers and Dangers, All Alone, Unarmed and Without Supplies in a Deep Forest

PULL IT LIKE CHESTY

PULL IT LIKE CHESTY

Life and Legacy of America's Most Decorated Marine, Chesty Puller

Author: Edgar Wollstone

Disclaimer

The content of this book is purely based on the facts learned through various sources. The author and publisher doesn't hold any responsibility based on accuracy, validity, and reliability for the given content. This content is based on the writer's perspective and imagination and doesn't mean to criticize anyone on a personal level. The author and publisher have strived their best to bring forth this amusing content for a wonderful reading experience.

Dedication

At the Feet of Lord

Acknowledgments

Sincerely thankful to everyone for their wholehearted support in making this book a reality.

Book Contents

Gruff Face in the Marine Corps History: The Strong Chesty Puller

Lewis Burwell "Chesty" Puller

The United States Marine Corps has a dedicated and venerated image that has always shone brightly in history. He is a decorated presence in the annals of the Corps. Having performed well in three wars and two counterattacks, he has a role that no one else can replace, with five Navy Crosses added to his fortune. Lewis Burwell Puller is the name of the figure who with a strong presence of mind, never stumbled, never prepared to fall, and with meticulous energy, carefully traced the steps of the battlefield. Most people know him as Chesty Puller. The following are the events that made the visage of Chesty Puller the focus of society: Battle of Guadalcanal, Battle of Chosin Reservoir, Korean War, World War II, and Pacific War.

Chapter 1: Vigorous element in defense

Primary moves

Born in West Point, Virginia, the son of Matthew Puller and Martha Puller, Lewis Burwell Puller, did not want to enter a resistant life. It was quite coincidentally and unhappily that he came to that field. Puller had to face the death of his father when he was only ten years old. His younger days went on as he read the stories of the heroes of the American Civil War and watched Thomas "Stonewall" Jackson with respect. In 1916, he longed to join the United States Army in the Border War (Punitive Expedition to seize Mexican leader Pancho Villa) with Mexico. But he was too young. Therefore, parental consent could not be obtained from his mother at the required stage. In the absence of his father, it was often his duty to look after the family. Thus, from the age of 10, along with his studies, he began to find a way of earning a living. He spent the rest of his free time going to the local warfront amusement park to sell crabs and also working as a pulp mill worker.

It was when he finished high school that they began to hear the utterances of World War I in the United States. At that time he decided to join the Virginia Military Institute. He was 17 at that time. He joined there as a state cadet. He later received financial assistance in return for his service. Puller did not rest in the summer either. An ordinary student, he burnt out time at the Reserve Officer Training Corps Camp in New York. It would be the last time he would turn his face away from the sounds of gunfire.

To the world of Marines

In April 1917, there was a rapid jump of U.S. into World War I. In such a situation, Puller became too busy and could not concentrate on his studies in that agitated atmosphere. He once too happened to watch the U.S. Marines' performance at Belleau Wood. Inspired by that, he left the Virginia Military Institute and then in 1918, he made his first steps into the Marine Corps. After completing his elemental training from Paris Island, South Carolina, made the wait meaningful and he got an appointment to officer candidate school. He then passed the course in Quantico, Virginia. When the conflict was over, he had acquired a commission. Puller was commissioned as a second lieutenant on June 16, 1919. He didn't leave the States. He was demoted to reserves.

Haiti days

Yet he did not want to say goodbye to military life. Therefore, on June 30, he embarked on another journey in the Marines as a man of corporal rank. In the heat of the U.S. invasion in Haiti, he resigned to attend the Marine-led gendarmerie by wearing officially the uniform of lieutenant, resigned and re-registered as a private individual for his active participation. Within five years he made a few minor interventions against farm guerrillas (Cacos rebels).

Major Alexander Vandegrift

Organized under an agreement signed between the U.S. and Haiti, the gendarmerie was staffed by American officers, mostly Marines and Haitian soldiers. During his time in Haiti, Puller worked tirelessly to recover his commission. And he served as adjutant to Major Alexander Vandegrift. He failed in the second round as a Marine officer candidate. He was unwilling to bow down in the face of defeat. Attempts continued. Eventually his efforts achieved success. In March 1924, he earned a permanent commission on his third attempt.

The stage where the achievements begin to be rewarded

The next four years were a crucial juncture in the marine life of Chesty Puller, a combatant. Puller's legs moved through various barracks leading from the East Coast to Pearl Harbour. Puller was deployed to Nicaragua in 1928 as part of the U.S. effort to support the government of Pres. Adolfo Diaz. For the first eighteen months he was seen in the guise of a frustrated staff officer. But in the end he made his initial mark as commander of the only unit of the Marine-led Guardia National which did not try to defend a city. The arrival of Puller in Central America was greeted with another experiment. There he fought the bandits for two years.

In the following years, Cesar Augustino Sandino's combative pursuit of the traitors led to many battles, famous for fearlessness, and finally to the nickname "Chesty". After ten months of extensive training in the Company Officers Course at the U.S Army Infantry School in Fort Benning, Georgia, Puller was ready for his second duty trip to Nicaragua in July 1932. The day after Christmas night of 1936, or five days before the end of the U.S. intervention, on December 26, Puller led a Guardia unit in one of the greatest successes of disturbances at EI Sauce.

Puller' experience in the guerrilla war while fighting the Caco rebels in Haiti set him up well for the Second Nicaraguan Campaign. During this time, there occurred a series of false propaganda among the Nicaraguan rebels. Sandinista rebels who were at war with the then U.S-backed government, were enemies of the National Guard force he went to train.

The Navy Cross compliment he earned during this campaign led Puller to "lead his army to five successful interventions against the Armed Forces", during which time he was nicknamed "EI Tiger" by the Nicaraguan armies. Amidst the same campaign, after two years of harsh fighting, Puller's patrol of 40 was ambushed and strategically attacked by an army of 150 rebels. In that situation, the reflex action from Puller extinguished the intensity to some extent. But they could not be completely relieved. As his quick and aggressive reply and tactics trampled the enemy, in which a bullet aimed at Puller was passed by him and it shot the man behind him, he lost two of his power, including the mentioned man, and was able to save the remaining population. Before returning to their shelter in Jinotega, he and his men hid twice in the same patrol, and in the meantime he received the Second Navy Cross for his courage and effort, spreading more sweetness to his achievements.

Maybe everyone should think that he will have a rest with this. By pouring water on those hopes and the dreams of enemies, he extinguished their coals of expectations and again excitedly stepped forward, disguised as the next brave warrior in the battlefield. That re-entry may have marked another historic moment. Far from their major themes, Puller continued to fight for American purposes for another three decades. There was another transformation of the energetic fighter that everyone could see.

Interventions in China

Puller's battleground for the next three years was China. The assignment that brought him to China was from 1933 to 1936. There he was in charge of the Marine detachment at USS Augusta under Captain Chester Nimitz and headed the famous

House Marines in Beijing. As the last days of his missions there approached, Puller was elevated to the position of captain in February 1936. He went back to America later that year to begin teaching assignment in The Basic School for the freshly commissioned or designated Marine officers. He began his three-year career as a tactical trainer on an advanced occasion for the officer corps. His lessons on the topic "small wars" may be needed later for a critical generation of Marine leaders or it will influence them. Days later, destiny arranged a journey again for him to the land of China. The goal was to assign him to new tasks. The U.S. Army Command and General Staff College in Fort Leavenworth, Kansas denied admission, and Puller again ordered China. He reached in July 1939 and resumed his duties as commander of Marine detachment in Augusta from where had stopped halfway. Chesty Puller's first expedition to China was able to make significant changes there. The second Sino-Japanese war began two years ago, with Japanese troops capturing most of China's ports and most of its major cities. The United States remained neutral in that strife, and the Japanese initially made small attempts to hamper the lives of foreigners in the Shanghai International Settlement, a de facto-controlled treaty port for Western governments. Puller became a member of the 4th Marine in Shanghai. In August 1940, he was upgraded to the rank of major. In the following years, some sights appeared in front of his naked eyes, as he saw the German armies consolidate its power in Western Europe and afterwards pounced on the Soviet Union. As rigidity gained strength in the Pacific, American military power in China waned and in August 1941,

Puller returned to the United States and made an assignment with the newly founded 1st Marine Division.

In the wrath of World War II

The United States felt that the time had come for a dispute with Japan. So while the United States was busy preparing for it, Puller received the command of the First Battalion. As things progressed, on December 7, 1941, a barrage of weapons and gun fires began to pierce Pearl Harbour. After the attack on Pearl Harbour started to hit the shores of peace, it attracted the U.S. into World War II and Puller gained his first experience on the American armies-led war ground. In May 1942, Puller and the 7th Marines set foot in Samova to shield Japan's attempt to sever the sea route between the U.S. and Australia. In a temporary rank of lieutenant colonel, Puller trained his troops for the ensuing battle they should have to face.

The first major Allied attack of the Pacific War began on August 7, 1942, with an amphibious landing at Guadalcanal in the southern Solomon Islands. Arriving at the 7th Marines on September 18, Puller's 1st Battalion began war patrolling the very next day to strengthen the still weak American beachhead. Puller had personally planned to save part of his encircled battalion after making an amphibious landing behind the foes during the Second Battle of Matanikau. From October 24 to 26, 1942, the nation was ravaged with torrential rain of sadness and destruction due to the Battle of Henderson Field. He got his third Navy Cross in that battle. Perhaps such a clash would have taken place to get that recognition into his hands. The path or venue for it may have been created in this way. Puller's body was bloodied by the Japanese machine gun and artillery shell that fell on his command post on November 8. But none of that could defeat the warrior. The atmosphere was disturbed by the fiery stench of blood and dust all around. In its aftereffect, the number of still bodies and wounded beings was inaccurate. An approximate figure is given. Officers of the 1st Battalion witnessed a 50% mortality rate in just eight weeks at Guadalcanal. The mortality rate of enrolled men was close to 30%.

Their strength diminished due to fighting and terrible illness, and in December 1942, the 7th Marines got relief and warmth through an Army regiment. After a brief hiatus from a few days of peace in Australia, Puller who later served as an executive officer of the regiment, landed respectfully on December 26, 1943 at Cape Gloucester in northwest New Britain. Once again it was time to add something to his series of achievements. Puller shortly commanded two battalions that lost commanders in a fierce battle. This led to the arrival of the fourth Navy Cross in search of him. On February 1, 1941, he was raised to the grade of temporary colonel. In September 1944, he took charge as commander of the 1st Marines for the attack against Peleliu. Given the toughest project-to capture Umurbrogol Ridge, the backbone of the enemy's stronghold - he had to lose more than half his men. Criticism that causes pain or resentment in which the major share of which is injustice or misrepresentation will dim the light of his reputation to a dark shade.

Battle of Peleliu on September 15, 1944

Sometimes in between these events, they were again at war with Japan in Papua New Guinea. His calm and cool demeanour, despite standing strong against a series of bombardments from the enemy side, gave him a different appearance in front of everyone at the time and made him more famous. It was because he maintained such a brawny attitude that the fourth Navy Cross was secured in his hands for the defence of the line. Not only with those characteristics he was able to achieve that accomplishment, but also Puller's valorous and unshakeable leadership was also an important factor for him to attain it. Coming forward with orders to attack, he immediately ignored the commander of the deep-rooted firm at the front and issued an order to go on the stalled progress. He dared the enemy to open fire on his army, and he enjoyed complete success in overcoming the Japanese position and advancing the American army quickly.

Puller in the background of Korean War

Gradually the island began to be safe. Puller then thought of a return. Returned to the U.S. and decided to lead as an instructor or head of the Infantry Training Regiment at Camp Lejeune. He kept that responsibility securely until the end of the war in 1945. Even years after the brutal end of World War II, the world of Marines has not left him. He was overseeing several commands, comprising the 8th Reserve District, Marine Barracks at Pearl Harbour.

Among those who knew his true potential, there was no change in his status. Like one problem after one another, the next one slowly began to loft up its head. Familiar to all, it was the Korean War that broke out on June 25, 1950 with a terrifying sound. When the Korean War began to intensify and the 1st Marine Division had to be speedily restored on a wartime basis, Major General O.P. Smith selected Puller for appointment. He led his old regiment through the brave amphibious attack on Inchon, the brutal street fighting in Seoul, the hurricane's frozen weather, and the constant Chinese humanitarian attack on the Chosin Reservoir Campaign.

Puller was awarded the fifth Navy Cross for his selfless service in Chosin. He also holds the record for being the only Marines in history to achieve the country's second highest military decoration award. The Army's Distinguished Service Cross also found a place in his attainments. For ten days, as the days of 1951 February moved close to its end and the new hopes of March began to dawn, Puller, who then held the chair of brigadier general and assistant division commander, set out with Smith to lead the division. Smith was conscious about Chesty's constraints. In addition, he maintained control of the division's reserve unit, and also knew that Puller wanted to bring his entire grab into battle at the beginning of a war. The Navy Cross that reached him through this was the fifth and final. Protecting American outposts from North Korean invaders at sub-zero temperatures, Puller re-deployed his forces properly, exposing those he commanded to enemy fire and artillery. As a result of his excellence in landings, the Silver Star and the second Legion of Merit shone brightly in his hands.

Chapter 2: Raising head in the crowd

Chesty Puller during the Korean War

Many of them have doubts as to why Chesty Puller deserves all the high positions as he adorned the role of command of various Marine Divisions and also served in the rank of Lieutenant General. Marines are often taught to imitate the best traits of those who have proven themselves to be heroes, who have shown extraordinary performance, and who are fearless leaders. Chesty was a perfect idol with the qualities that Marines want to copy.

Danny Strand, Director of Marine Corps Logistics Base Barstow's Safety and Emergency Services, has always been a talkative person when it comes to discussions about Puller. In his opinion, Chesty Puller's experience shows that college education is not necessary to lead the Marines. He added his guess that Puller was one among them at some point and therefore he would understand what they were going through. In Strand's assumption, that's the reason why he is everyone's favourite image. Many have attributed Puller's exemplary leadership qualities to his ability to connect with the Marines he led. Puller's heroic adventure stories described above have made other Marines understand why he always remains a colourful portrait. There are many fictional and nonfictional tales about Puller's valour. His later fame and respect was ten times greater than his bravery during his service. Another guise of his maturity outside the war, his words, and deeds increased the number of his admirers. Strand said Puller maintained a higher standard than anyone he knew. Retired lieutenant colonel and his fellow mustang, an anonymous great personality, unveiled a small incident that evoked memories of his days. In his time, the casual discharge of their weapons cost twenty dollars. He was once fined one hundred dollars. Behind his reputation as a figure that attracts everyone, there are some features that make him unique and different in his style. Others may find it trivial and have common characteristics, but it's important who does it and how. Puller's approach to situations with common sense, seriousness and understanding always holds him in high esteem. His talent for handling any responsibility that comes his way with its completeness and positive attitude should be highlighted. He had a special calibre to carry his companions shoulder to shoulder. Puller earned the respect of those who served through the lessons he taught.

Chesty Puller was able to present an outstanding service that had never been seen or heard of before in the 20th century. His role in the culture of the Marines and the United States Army from his years in Haiti will be a lasting influence for decades, and the name "Chesty Puller" will forever shine brightly in history. Throughout his career, Chesty followed a particular motivation. It was as follows. He was also as afraid of him as the average man. But the thought that it was for his men forced him so strongly to be firm in his stand so that he remoulded fearlessly himself for that purpose. He motivated himself to fight for unity without giving time to selfish thoughts to dominate. He probably always remembered the proverb "unity is strength."

Post wars

Disappointed with the behaviour of the war in Korea and being desperate for some bad preparations of certain military units, Puller went back to the States and was trapped in front of the media. He openly uncovered what was in his mind. It went on to create controversial headlines in a nutshell. By then, Puller was one of the most colourful, Bright, and determined figures in the history of the Marine Corps according to different media. Again, many media outlets described his commendable services in proud words. His bitter experience so far could not pull him back from arguing strongly for rigorous training, and his mission to command the only brigade in the Corps did not go astray in half. Following the tour as the head of an amphibious coaching team, he reached the high position as the major general and in July 1954 was assigned to the commander of the 2nd Marine Division in North Carolina.

Chapter 3: Inspiring attributes of Puller

Whoever the Marine, when they come to that area, they try to copy their role model, Chesty Puller. Thus an image was always reserved for him. He is a key portrait relatable to all Marines. "Marine's Marine" is an adjective that was once given to him by society. Time has predicted that prediction to be true. Several roles were simmering in his hands at the same time or at different times.

There are a number of reasons why Chesty Puller, who might have to fit into the hectic schedules of an ordinary life, was brought to the pinnacle of a Marine Corps legend. He later spread those impetuses as his quotes when reached the top.

The motto he learns is to lead like a Marine by example. He lived with his men regardless of the value of status or anything else. There was nothing wrong with the officers' attire. He also spent time with private people, and engaged in his own mess between official deeds. His career days show that he can deal with personal problems and formal mishmash together without being bored. He, too, raised his hands and vehemently denied the comforts which his men could not attain in the battle. In training, he carried his own packs and bedding roll as he marched towards his battalion. He lived as one of them with the common people who stayed with him. He did not show any pride in his power. The light of wonder and joy shone in the eyes of those who were watching all his activities. He was also involved in a 28-day patrol through New Britain. In the meanwhile, he refused the natives who approached him to take his pack, which was shifted along with the essentials. In this simplicity of his, the love of others for him increased again. Like the men around him, he also followed a monotonous diet of "K" rations. He adopted the same method in other facilities. When his colleagues lived in minimal amenities he was not able to survive on improvised means. He tried his best to practice the manner of equality. At night, or amidst the battle, he looked for a place in an abandoned native hut or deck or bare floor, where he wanted to lay his head to take a short rest. The natives were ready to make a mattress out of banana leaves for him where there were lesser facilities. But he refused it. There are many fictional stories about that fighter with extraordinary fighting prowess.

Tales behind "Chesty"

Chesty Puller is commonly known as "Chesty" or "Puller". The "Puller" came from his real name Lewis Burwell Puller, and it made it easier for everyone to call him. There are many stories behind the origin of the nickname "Chesty". Let's look at one or two that are more prevalent. It is said that he got that famous nickname because of his big piercing chest. The myth was that the original had been shot and that the new chest was a steel plate. It may not actually be practical, but since it is a legendary fable it does not make sense to check the reality. Such stories may have spread because he faced anything with a firm heart and courage. Explanations have been heard from some quarters that the old Marine expression "chesty" also means cocky. One group claims that he developed his chest from the horns above the trumpet of war.

Chesty Puller is a highly respected personality because of his performances overflowed in incidents with Marines' sacrifices and exploits such as World War II, Guadalcanal & Peleliu, and his past accomplishments in owning five Navy Crosses. His role as commander of the 1st Marines, which prompted his landing at Inchon on September 15, 1950, earned him the Silver Star. In the same year, the Army's Distinguished Service Cross came into his hands for his services from November 29 to December 5. The fifth Navy Cross was also acquired as a result of the Battle of Chosin Reservoir held from 5 to 10 December. With all this, he became known as the most decorated Marine in history. Although all this has been mentioned many times, if we narrow down to one topic which is what inspires us from his experiences, it will all be incomplete without the efforts and achievements that has just said.

He worked both as an officer and as an enlisted person. Puller witnessed World War I and World War II with his own eyes. He was commissioned as a 2nd Lieutenant in the background of the First World War. As the war cooled, he was moved to an inactive status and given the rank of corporal. He was re-enlisted as a private in accordance with his bad attitude. He was sent to Haiti to fight the Caco Rebels for violently displacing the U.S - sponsored Haitian government. His valour and achievements in the battlefield gave him rapid successes and promotions. By the time he sailed for Nicaragua in 1930, the position of Lieutenant was reached again to him. Puller's legend greatly influenced young men. They were impressed by him, who survived through the woods and other difficult paths and conditions. His men knew that he had their backs wounded in many battles like them.

Puller won a good reputation in front of his superiors as a person who showed no political intrigues. Everyone had respect and love for him as a person who kept a straight forward attitude. The respect bestowed on him by his people for his outstanding service in warfare earned him the nation's highest award, the Medal of Honour.

Marine who conveyed messages through quotes

It's doubtful whether he has ever treated anyone more friendlily. He has established a good place among all with his admirable deeds, but sometimes he was a man with a rough space. He may have become so because of the seriousness of the missions he undertook. He lives with these actions and his quotes forever. The U.S. has many writers of its own, but he has attracted attention with his coolest style of sayings.

In 1942, an incident occurred while Chesty Puller was discharging his responsibilities. A pipe was smoked during a bomb blast in Guadalcanal. At the time he was a lieutenant colonel and commander of the 1st battalion, 7th Marine Regiment at Guadalcanal. He was the only person with earlier experience of war, and none of the men with him acted with false intelligence. Thus came the stage to test the leadership quality of Lieutenant colonel Puller. The reason for the phase to test his leadership was because the bombardment took place on the first night of their attempts. Puller ran through the ups and downs of the line. At the same time he instructed his men to take cover. As it almost began to see its end, Puller walked along the lines while pulling a pipe. He gave his Marines a comforting warning of their final victory.

The presence of Chesty Puller has been identified in multiple films. HBO's "The Pacific" was the best representation of it. In it, Puller's most notable role was played by William Sadler. The John Ford documentary on his life, titled, "Chesty: "A Tribute to a Legend", in John Wayne's narration, brought his life to its fullest. The following is another example of the sincere fighting spirit of the combatant Chesty Puller. He skilfully used his Regiment as a Division rear guard in the continuous firing and other attacks from Koto-ri to Hungman. He resisted two fierce enemy attacks that posed a serious threat to the unit's security. It was a huge setback for those eyes that spit the flames of enmity. He also personally supervised the maintenance and rapid evacuation of all accidents. His fighting spirit to jump over the barriers whatever coming in his path is his ever positive aspect and that leads everyone towards him. In his unwavering determination, he inspired his men to make heroic efforts to hold on tightly their positions and ensure the safety of valuable equipment that the enemy might lose. His gifted leadership, extraordinary courage, and courageous dedication to duty in the face of extreme obstacles are shining brightly in front of the high credits of Colonel Puller and the United States Naval Service.

Chapter 4: Here and there

Let's go through some combats that found the presence of a trooper who made life eventful with about 37 years of service.

Chesty Puller's main battlefield was World War II.

Battle of Guadalcanal

US Marines during the Guadalcanal campaign

Do you have any idea when you hear the name Guadalcanal? This was a key point in Puller's career. You can see an island located in the South Pacific Ocean. It is Guadalcanal.

The Battle of Guadalcanal was a major conflict between the United States and Japan during the Second World War. This is the setting that is part of the Solomon Islands situated to the northeast of Australia. At first General Alexander Vandegrift and later General Alexander Patch led the U.S. forces in that erratic flow. There was a faction that was a major strength in that war, the naval forces. Their head was Admiral Richmond Turner. General Hitoshi Imamura and Admiral Isoroku Yamamoto led the army from the front of the opposition side, Japan. The attack on Pearl Harbour was the first to plunge everyone into the abyss of misery and devastation. Its aftereffect was the Japanese move to wipe out most of Southeast Asia. Until about 1942, most of the South Pacific including the Philippines, were in their hands. In the aftermath, they began to raise threats against the U.S. ally of Australia. The United States did not sit idly by. During the interval of Pearl Harbour, finally they mobilized the forces from the Pacific to retaliate against Japan and the U.S. entered the war ground. The search for locations suitable for their attack ended when they found themselves in the Guadalcanal. They once built an air base there to assail New Guinea.

Chesty Puller on Guadalcanal in September, 1942

When the marines took over the island, it was on August 7, 1942, that the war began, with eyes burning with rage. The small islands of Florida and Tulagi, just north of the Guadalcanal, were the first to catch the attention of their enemy. Their next aim was the Guadalcanal. Thus the whole army thronged the Guadalcanal by shouting the sounds of war. The marines took control of the air base, much to the surprise of the Japanese.

If you think Japanese will get tired of that then that thought is wrong. They were not ready to give up quickly. The battlefront got prepared for the next phase. Victory in a naval battle on Savo Island was on their side. They sank the cruiser of four Allied forces. And they isolated the U.S. Marines at Guadalcanal. Then they brought reinforcements to increase their strength to bring the island under their control. For over six months the war raged on in the fires of terror. The U.S. was able to save the island from adversaries by planning and taking actions for it during the day to bomb the upcoming Japanese ships. The power of the Japanese began to wane slowly. Later they somehow found small ships in which they landed at night. Attempts were made to send more troops. By mid-November, the Japanese had mobilized 10,000 soldiers and moved the reins of a major offensive. There was a fierce battle going on, but the Japanese's moves could not be pushed forward by force. The excitement of the U.S. increased and became more robust when they saw the rival team weakening. Eventually the Japanese were forced to withdraw. When the foeman becomes feeble, naturally the success will be to the other side. At that point, the United States raised the banner of victory in the battle. The fight ended with the U.S.

gaining total control of the island on February 9, 1943. It was here that the Japanese first had to drink the bitter water of defeat in a war. It seriously affected the morale of both sides. Approximately 31,000 soldiers' lives and 38 ships were added to the list of irreparable losses for the Japanese. The loss to Allies was 29 ships and the lives of 7,100 soldiers.

Battle of Chosin Reservoir

The presence of the Marine Chesty Puller was mainly spotted in the 1950s at the Battle of Chosin Reservoir, a major part of the Korean War. It was something that lasted only about a month. Its heat lasted from 17 November to 13 December 1950.

Major General Oliver P. Smith (1st Marine Division), Major Douglas MacArthur, and Major General Edward Almond (X Corps) were the ones who gave courage to the United Nations from the forefront. General Song Shi-Lun led their force for China.

Battle of Chosin Reservoir

The United States Command under the leadership of the United States was conquered by South Korea after the attack on them. Next there started to see an invasion of China. It was only after several warnings to the United Nations that they entered this arena. China's attacks on the United Nations Command have continued unabated, forcing them to withdraw. The end of the war was to create a stalemate of separating Korea into 38th parallel. Thus the clashes took place within Korea itself. The equilibrium of the country was vibrated by the partition of North Korea and South Korea. North Korea invaded and occupied most of South Korea's 38th parallel. The South Korean army cleared out to Busan, also known as the port city and the second largest city in South Korea. With the intervention of the United Nations Army, they landed in Incheon and captured Seoul. The United Nations' dominance in North Korea has increased and there have been aggressive movements to the Yalu River on China's border. Chinese forces have penetrated many of North Korea's secret hideouts. Mao Zedong, the Chinese communist revolutionary and also the founder of the People's Republic of China, had decided to execute plans to use weapons against the United Nations in the Second Phase Offensive.

Following the victory of the Korean War on October 25, 1950, the United Nations forces were seen to be shut down, while the Communist Chinese forces began to cross the border. The UN troops, who were extending their branches, were severely pressed and repulsed by the opponents to stay away from the front. Unable to support each other, the US X Corps isolated in North-eastern Korea. These units, which surrounded the Chosin Reservoir, consisted of troops of the 7th Infantry Division and

1st Marine Division. As the movement progressed rapidly, the People's Liberation Army's (PLA) Ninth Group Army blocked the advance of the X Corps and clustered the UN troops at Chosin. Almond commanded Major General Oliver P. Smith, one of the captains of the 1st Marine Division, to draw back the combat again to the coast.

When it was November 26, the climate got worse for them. Smith's men were troubled by the numbing cold and choppy weather. The next day the stage was set for another attack. They stormed against the 5th and 7th Marines from their spot near Yudam-ni located on the west bank of the reservoir. They earned some success in opposition to the PLA forces in the area. Over the next three days, they successfully protected their positions at Yudam-ni and Hagaru-ri against the man-made attacks on the 1st Marine Division in China. It was at this point that they needed the involvement of the Marine Chesty Puller. On November 29, Smith came into touch with Colonel "Chesty" Puller, commander of the 1st Marine Regiment in Koto-ri, and asked him to assemble a task force to re-open the road from there to Hagaru-ri. Obeying these instructions, Puller organized a force composed of Lieutenant Colonel Douglas B. Drysdale's Royal Marines Battalion (41 Independent Commando), 31st Infantry (B Company), 1st Marines (G Company) and other rear grade troops. Including 900 men, a 140-vehicle task force left at morning 9:30 on the 29th with the command of Drysdale. The road to Hagaru-ri was pushed upwards and the task force fainted due to the ambush of the Chinese soldiers. Drysdale fought in a locale known as "Hell Fire Valley" and was strengthened by tankers sent by Puller. With all their might, the men of Drysdale fired a gauntlet of fire, and most of the 41 Commando, with G Company and tanks arrived at Hagaru-ri. At thc time of attack, B Company and 31st Infantry were separated and isolated on the road. All of its consequences were prepared by the lamenting feast of regular sights. While one group was killed or others captured, a third category escaped to Koto-ri. As the Marines battled west, the 31st Regimental Combat Team of the 7th Infantry was wrestling with pains to regain life on the troubled shores of the reservoir. On December 2, some of the survivors of the unit reached the Marine lines of Hargaru-ri. While retaining his current position in Hagaru-ri, Smith asked the 5th and 7th Marines to leave the area around Yudam-ni and unite the rest. The Marines entered Hagaru-ri on December 4 during a confrontation as they stood in barefoot for three days on boiling coals. After two days, Smith's command began to fight back, demanding that they wanted to return to Koto-ri. As they moved towards Hungnam, the Marines and other elements of the X Corps continued to attack.

A golden feather fell on the success of the campaign on December 9. The achievement was the construction of a bridge over the 1,500 ft. grudge between Koto-ri and Chinhung-ni utilizing pre-made bridge sections abandoned by the U.S. Air Force. December 11 was the end of everything and the downfall of the enemies.

There is no guarantee that it was a complete success in every sense. However, when one evaluates it as a whole, they can realize that the departure from the Chosin Reservoir is a milestone in the history of the U.S. Marine Corps. During the fighting, the Marines and other UN troops effectively destroyed or wore out seven Chinese divisions that sought to hinder their growth. Looking at the gap left by the Marines in the campaign, everyone knows that 836 deaths and 12,000 wounded occurred. Most of the rest were injured in the scorching heat and freezing cold. The U.S. Army lost 2,000 lives and 1,000 wounded. The emptiness on the Chinese side is inaccurate, but the average estimate says it was between 19,202 and 29,800. Arriving at Hungnam, the veterans of the Chosin Reservoir were moved out as part of a larger amphibious operation to rescue UN troops from north-eastern Korea.

Next chapter of life and entry of unexpected rival

He entered into the area of defence from a very young age and worked in front of the services day and night without any rest. After all such activities, when he started wanting a relaxed life, his physical condition started to worry him. While active in armed missions, he was occasionally visited by high blood pressure and heart problems. For him, it was like an uninvited guest was knocking on the door and making a loud noise. So he did not mind it in the midst of all that hustle and bustle. Sickness waited for an opportunity and expressed that anger to him while he was at rest. He had suffered a stroke after a long examination in an infantry battalion one day when the sun was at its extreme fury and the earth was scorched by its heat. It took him to the hospital bed. While acquiring a little relief, there were attempts to jump out of there. Again he fought hard to stay in the Corps against any enemy. But still, as always, health did not give him the green signal. It showed the red signal in the form of medical science. The Navy medical board assumed that he was no longer fit to work with the old vigour. In October 1955, he was pressured to resign from that area with the post of lieutenant general honorary rank.

In 1962, Burke Davis, a historical writer, exposed to light the book, *Marine! The Life of Chesty Puller*, a semi-autobiographical element of the life of Chesty Puller, a marine magician. His displeasure intensified his prejudice against staff officers, and he sharpened his addiction to his confession. Also, the influence of that book was also very strong. Puller chose Saluda to live his later quiet days, marked only by his testimony in favour of hard training during the sensational McKeon trial at Parris Island in 1956.

Chesty Puller opened a new chapter in his life, hoping for a quiet life without war and affray. At first, it was not difficult for that Marine to lead a life as he had imagined. Lewis B. "Chesty" Puller married Virginia Montague Evans on November 13, 1937 as a better half to share his days ahead. Virginia McCandlish announced her birth as their eldest kid, welcoming them to the stage of parents for the first time in just a few years of their union. Immersed in the innocence and associated play of that child, the family became sweeter a few years later with the birth of Lewis Burwell Puller.

Chesty Puller & Virginia Montague Evans

His son Lewis Puller also followed in his father's footsteps, went through many critical stages like his father, and had to accept injuries. He became a Marine infantry officer. In 1968, after stepping on a baited-trap cannon shell in Vietnam, he found horrible wounds on his body. Chesty died in October 1971 due to uncontrolled entry of strokes in his life. With 37 years of dedicated service, Chesty Puller has achieved the distinction of being the most decorated Marine in American history.

Jr. Puller wrote the Pulitzer Prize winning autobiography of title, Fortune Son, in 1991 as a tribute to his father and to be all familiar with their bond, and eventually he accepted death with his own hands in 1994.

Chesty Puller was a man who, at a very young age, overcame the fences of dissatisfaction at home and rose to prominence as a Marine. His perseverance and constant calmness and determination to bring to fruition any action he undertakes, and his legacy as the uncrowned King of the United States Marine Corps, Chesty Puller will remain in mythology forever. He contributed 37 years of active service as a Marine from 1918 to 1955, during that long time he achieved a space of his own in the pages of history. He overcame all the combats that followed him one after the other, holding on to his courage and succeeding without the will to give up.

Chesty Puller as a Major General

In sum

"Chesty Puller" is the name that always shines with innovation in the corridors that U.S. Marines pass through. In a sudden morning unexpectedly, the mind of a soldier who wanted to go to war started to follow him. When his father's untimely death and at a very young age he had to carry a portion of the family burden on his shoulders, he had to pull that wish from his front to the side for a while. Puller knew, however, that he would become the largest Marine in history. His strength is the confidence that he always held in his grip and the determination that he always sharpened without losing his valour. He was a tenacious person who emerged from a heritage with small connection to the defence field and later turned his life in the same direction. General George S. Patton was his cousin, and that was the link for him towards the area of resistance. His dedicated service may have shaken Puller. He soon moulded himself physically and even more mentally for a military future. Thus out of a firm desire to take part in the war, his entry into the Virginia Military Institute and his subsequent actions were the first step towards his goal. But for Puller, the roads to the army were full of thorns, which sowed the seeds of despair. The textbooks did not cut for his dream of a military career. His only passion when he was in school was always in his rifle range. It did not comfort him as he was a hunter at a young age. After being in inactive duty he did not consider his officer position as worthy and expressed his disappointment in that way. So he risked his officer position and joined the expansive world of the Marine Corps. He was nicknamed "Chesty" for the way his chest swelled. The recognition he later received was proof that the challenge he undertook was not in vain.

He believed in a dream that had once unexpectedly taken root in him. For that he did not see or notice the differences between day and night. He had an exact route map of where he was going and where it was ending. So he obeyed that direction precisely through his hard work. The new Chesty Puller could not have been designed without clear goals and resolution. Looking at the lessons of the Marine Corps, they teach that Puller was the greatest Marine. Only a few people knew why he joined the Corps. He left the Virginia institute in 1918 and enlisted in the Marine Corps. It was at that time the United States' participation in World War I came to the fore. While he was in officer training, the coals of that war were extinguished by a slight wind blowing at the first buds of Puller's desire. While he achieved the rank of second lieutenant in the year 1919, he slowly withdrew from active duty, holding on to its tail. It was then that issues in Haiti affected him. Puller was willing to do anything to make his dreams of becoming a soldier come true. Whatever risks he was taking, it was all right for him. He did not want to see the Americans fall, and closed his eyes tightly. His mind raced to fight as one of them with his men who were constantly shedding tears, blood, and sweat. He did not even try to divert his attention from the Marines until death approached him. As his life began to resent him, he had to physically stay away from the U.S. Marine Corps, where his life and soul were. When the disease slowly manifested itself in a false silence, he begged for a return to service. He got silent there too.

There is no need to wonder if Marine history is categorized as before and after Chesty Puller. This is because there is only one Chesty Puller equal to the Chesty Puller. It is impossible for someone to replace him. The attitude he shows towards his services is the same integrity that most people show in their field of work. But those who know him intimately will understand the difference in what he does or the uniqueness within it. His qualities of honesty and loyalty to the Marine Corps were never abandoned until his death. Because he loved and respected his country so much that he was even willing to die for the country. It was there that the patriot within him woke up. It was unbelievable to those who did not know the stories that he was able to fight and survive in those battles of his career where blood flowed and wounds prepared their playing field. Concerns over whether he could breathe his last in his favourite place where his soul breathes Oxygen, or whether he would be able to do whatever he wanted at the Marine Corps until the last particle of life was removed from his body, overwhelmed him. However, instead of waiting for the last days with his arms outstretched, he longed to fight and die on the battlefield until its arrival, as if to defeat that destiny. Before he died, his last request was that he should have to die on the battlefield and fall in the warfare with his men. His experience like this will be chapters that are electrifying to others. His life shows that if one can have optimism, a firm dream, determination and a will to work for it, they will achieve their goal. When everyone sees him at first sight, they can see the glowing face of a general on the weight of the medals he won. But those close to him will understand the truth of the stories of his leadership and sacrifice hidden behind that glow. Readers who are trying to get to know him better, in which Puller has achieved a totality of his efforts and are seeing him as medals sticking to his chest, may sometimes try to extract new meanings similar to his nickname "'Chesty" from his appearance. There may be those who are jealous of the brilliance of his medals, and sometimes there are those who have no such thought at all. Maybe if there were people who thought so, then it would melt away if they sincerely look back at the realities behind all that came to him. Puller's moves influenced everyone and motivated them to do everything he did. He is a great leader who can set an example for others with his actions. Puller represents the Marines and is also a symbol of them. His transcendence from a private officer to a general with a three-star highlights his dedication to the country and men and his sincerity to duty. This is what led him to become an icon worshiped by the Marine Corps. For them, Chesty Puller is an imaginary face that gives qualities like strength, courage, and determination. The reply or a guide to the Marine Corps who finds it difficult to find a solution in every difficult situation is the way he is accustomed to. The honour, courage, and commitment that everyone realized through him were his possessions that Puller passed on to everyone.

Review Request

Eternally grateful for your recent purchase. We hope you love it! If you do, would you consider posting an online review? This helps us to continue providing great efforts and coherent growth.

Thank you in advance for your review and for being a preferred customer.

Don't miss out!

Visit the website below and you can sign up to receive emails whenever Edgar Wollstone publishes a new book. There's no charge and no obligation.

https://books2read.com/r/B-A-CXBO-RCGLC

BOOKS 2 READ

Connecting independent readers to independent writers.

Did you love *Pull It Like Chesty : Life and Legacy of America's Most Decorated Marine, Chesty Puller*? Then you should read *Antarctic Voyages : Daring Tales of Early Antarctic Explorations by Amundsen, Shackleton and Falcon Scott*[1] by Ted Harvey!

[2]

Robert Falcon Scott and Roald Amundsen, Explorers

Two men are on a race to the edge of the world but only one would return. English naval officer ***Robert Scott and Norwegian explorer Roald Amundsen*** *are on a race to the* ***South Pole****, but Nature would aid only one and abandon the other to die in a frozen grave forever. With all other continents already conquered, there was but just one that was left untouched and this was reason*

1. https://books2read.com/u/3ydweJ

2. https://books2read.com/u/3ydweJ

enough to initiate a race to the bottom of the world. But this race to be the first man on the South Pole can have only one heroic winner. Two men, equally competent, fired by the passionate quest to reach the South Pole before any man would, but only one returns home to tell tales of endurance, resilience, survival, and success, the other lies buried under ice in a frozen grave to this day. What could have brought about this stark difference of fate? Where did one succeed and the other falter? Will Norway's flag flutter triumphantly over the South Pole, or is it the British flag?

Ernest Shackleton, Explorer

It was an ominous day. We were reduced to helpless trespassers in a forbidding world. Nature with all her might seemed to make ribaldry of our fragile attempts at survival. There were times when we thought we saw God and Death, and some moments when we realized that both were the one and the same. Standing atop the drifting ice, it felt as though a giant was heaving in his deep slumber. The slightest stir would suffice to awaken the odious beast, the harbinger of our doom. It was on occasions like these that I felt a thousand words in the English vocabulary is not enough to express the overwhelming roller-coaster of emotions one experiences in an odyssey to the edge of the world. It was nothing short of a tryst with death and yet it is incredulous that in the tug of war with death, we, the puny human souls have managed to grab our lives from the very mighty jaws of death. The ocean was livid and her humongous waves that could rise to 50 feet height were crashing against our tiny lifeboat, determined to tear us apart. The heaven seemed to be in cahoots with her, it seemed to split into two. Her wrath was so fearsome and deadly, it seemed hell-bent to crush us like crushing ice with a gigantic hammer. Life, the game of all games was now proving to be a reckoning force; maybe it was because we were not just fighting for our lives alone, but for the lives of 22 fellow men stranded in the Elephant Island, that we just couldn't be defeated. They would be counting on our arrival, for a semblance of hope that they can go back home, alive. When ***Ernest Shackleton****, the great Anglo-Irish explorer embarked on Endurance in the year 1914 for a historic expedition to cross the Antarctic, he didn't know he was walking into the pages of history for reasons that he was unprepared for.*

This book on **Antarctica expeditions** narrates the best **survival stories** of, **polar expeditions**. In the realm of Antarctic expeditions, the three names that are written in letters of fire are that of the great explorer **Roald Amundsen, Robert Falcon Scott**, and the one and only **Ernest Shackleton**. Insurmountable fear, the great possibility of death, unbearable starvation, relentless uncertainties, debilitating seasickness, umpteen failures, and inexplicable sacrifice, all for an iota of joy and triumph at the end of a grueling journey to the edge of the world. This is what these young men signed up for before embarking on a treacherous journey to the world's driest, coldest, windiest regions on the earth.

Also by Edgar Wollstone

Chronicles of Spy Ladies

Miss Fatale - Greatest World War II Female Spy, In a Fly : Virginia Hall's Finger Prints over Allies' World War II Victory

Agent Sonya - The Lady of Espionage : Astounding Story of The Spy Ursula Kuczynski

Life & Legacy In a Fly

Churchill's Better Half - Clementine Churchill : Life and Legacy of Winston Churchill's Wife, Clementine Churchill, in a Fly

Sniper Chronicles

Simo Hayha - The Deadliest Sniper In Military History : War Story of The Deadliest Sniper In Military History, In a Fly

Lady Death - The Beauty With a Sniper : Fascinating Tale of Lyudmila Pavlichenko, The Deadliest Female Sniper in History

Carlos Hathcock - Vietnam's Most Wanted Sniper : The Sniper's Extraordinary Engagements During Vietnam War, in a Fly

Killing Silently : American Sniper Chris Kyle's Lethal Moments
Sniper of Vietnam War : The Shots of Marine Sniper Chuck Mawhinney, In a Fly
500+ Kills - Sniper Ivan Sidorenko : WWII Hero of the Soviet Union
Deadly Sniper Duels - The War Story of Controversial Duel Between The Soviet Sniper Expert Vasily Zaitsev And The Mysterious Top Nazi Sniper in WW2

Titan Fails

Titan Fails - Vietnam War : How & Why America Lost the Vietnam War

War Classics In a Fly

Battle of the Atlantic, in a Fly : Long 2,075 days of War in World War 2
Battle of Midway, WWII Naval Battle in a Fly : Captivating Read on the Motives, Strategies, Tactics and the Winning Events of the Decisive World War II Battle
Battle of Okinawa, in a Fly : A Chilling Epitome on the Bloodiest Battle in Pacific Theater of World War 2
D-DAY, in A Fly : Deceptive Operation Bodyguard, Gruesome Battle of Normandy and the Aftermath
American Civil War, in a Fly

World War II Military Operations

Operation Mincemeat : A WWII British Deception Operation
Laconia Incident - A High-Risk Military Rescue Operation of WWII Under The Line of Fire
Operation Vengeance - Killing Admiral Yamamoto : The Stunning Top Secret WWII Military Operation, In a Fly

Standalone

Maya Angelou's Life In a Fly : Retrospective Voyage Through the Life of Maya Angelou
Yoshie Shiratori, The Grand Jailbreaker : Heart-Touching Story of a Japanese Jailbreak Expert
Dawn After Twilight : Industrial Rising of Japan After WW2
Ben L Salomon, The Lone Machine Gunner : A Valiant Story from WW2, in a Fly
Manoeuvres, Shots and Drops - Dive Bomber Pilot Richard Halsey Best In World War 2
Hitler's Girls : Captivate Spy Stories of WWII Female Nazi Spies
Oppenheimer - The Atomic Intelligence : Inside The Brilliant Mind of Robert Oppenheimer, Father of The Atomic Bomb
Puerto Rican Rambo - Story of Jorge Otero Barreto, The Most Decorated U.S. Soldier Of The Vietnam War : Sergeant Rock, In a Fly
Pull It Like Chesty : Life and Legacy of America's Most Decorated Marine, Chesty Puller
The Dark Encounters in Vietnam : Spine-Chilling Horror Stories From Vietnam War
The Other Side of Agent Zigzag : Greatest Double Agent of World War II, Eddie Chapman, In a Fly

The Real Peaky Blinders : Gangster Story of The Actual Peaky Blinders, From Origin to Fall

Niihau Incident : When a Japanese Pilot After Pearl Harbor Attack Crash-Landed on a Hawaiian Island

The Bermuda Triangle of Transylvania, - Hoia Forest -

The Forgotten War Heroes of Vietnam War - Volume II : War Stories of William Pitsenbarger, William Maud Bryant & Jimmie E. Howard

The Forgotten War Heroes of Vietnam War - Volume I : War Stories of George “Bud” Day, Drew Dix, & Jay Vargas

WW2 in Meth - Battling Hallucinations, Enemy Soldiers and Dangers, All Alone, Unarmed and Without Supplies in a Deep Forest

Printed in the USA
CPSIA information can be obtained
at www.ICGtesting.com
LVHW012257050424
776557LV00002B/413